W9-AZM-281

No Mercy

ALSO BY LEE UPTON

The Invention of Kindness

No Mercy

LEE UPTON

THE ATLANTIC MONTHLY PRESS
NEW YORK

Published simultaneously in Canada
Printed in the United States of America
FIRST EDITION

Library of Congress Cataloging-in-Publication Data
Upton, Lee, 1953–
   No mercy / Lee Upton. — 1st ed.
   (The National poetry series)
   ISBN 0-87113-328-8
   I. Title.   II. Series.
PS3571.P46N6   1989   811'.54—dc20   89-6885

The Atlantic Monthly Press
19 Union Square West
New York, NY 10003

Design by Laura Hough

FIRST PRINTING

I would like to thank the following people:
Richard Buttny, Patricia Donahue, Sheila McNamee,
Tom Ham and Donald Revell.

The National Poetry Series
Tenth Annual Series—*1988*

The National Poetry Series was established in 1978 to publish five collections of poetry annually through five participating publishers. The manuscripts are selected by five poets of national reputation. Publication is funded by the Copernicus Society of America, James A. Michener, Edward J. Piszek, The Lannan Foundation and the five publishers—E. P. Dutton, Graywolf Press, Atlantic Monthly Press, Persea Books, Inc., and the University of Illinois Press.

—for Lana, Alice and Joe Upton

Contents

I

II

III

No Mercy

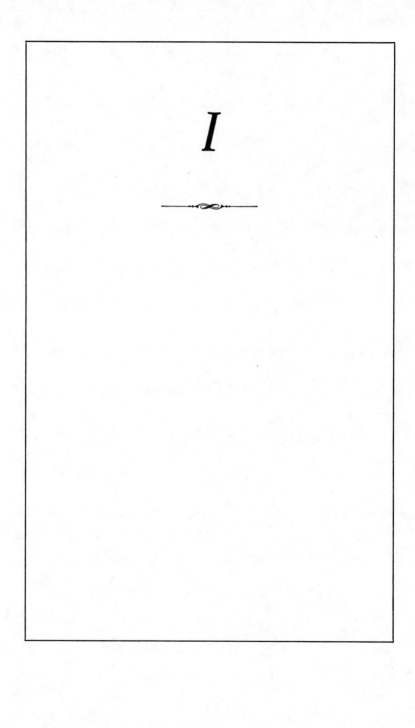

I

The Imagination of Flowers

Perennial snow on the mountain,
dragon's blood sedum, fever dew.
They are doing what
their kind do: crying,
Enter me I don't care.
As if the world turns
its lips around them
just as some of us will do
for some others. He's rich,
the man who watches the woman
raking around a plaster chicken. And
the woman, they say, is not quite
right. Making a plaster chicken at home
is all it looks like to him.
  In the morning the mist appears to break
the garden's ornamental bridge
as if someone cannot walk back
that way again.
In the stories of childhood,
those that make us happy,
someone is always caught
for good. She can't go back either.
That's justice: Someone else says
No. The world won't love you enough.
We might believe all this
but there is so much tenderness
in even that woman
raking around a chicken.
  When the man slides open the glass
doors, he walks to her. They stand quietly

as if waiting
for a story some flowers might tell
when they are very tired and about
to blow over the lawn.
Some of them believe there is
no snow and that it is a burden
only they can bear—to be beautiful.
For others, they do what they can:
The woman's hand is muscular and moving,
and the man, he has, he has
some lovely spotted money he waves
into all that racket
inside the woman's head.

Lee Upton

Scroll

A water stain nibbles at the side of a woman's mouth.
A rock that froths seems eaten into like a biscuit.
This world all curls up for us
into a black box with hinges.
We may visit the things that corrupt here
with evil about to tear everywhere around us,
a kind of thin bread.
The leering man will poison the fellow
whose face is already half-eaten, whose hands
are poking out of his jacket.
But the villain never reaches that man,
although when this all rolls up, I think of them closer,
the one the night sky to the other.
The villain looks down as if he'd only sop
the poor man's head with a sponge.
It helps me to see I can see this.
As if only a little of the poison goes into me,
to make me strong, to make me see.
The courtesan with her lovely white slab of a face
is about to shuffle off without jostling
the villain, making him spill.
Yet a little of the poison is sure to spill.
Like dew, it wets all these lips,
trembles on the tiny hairs on the backs of our hands.
I brush it across my own lips.
As if I brush lips with the devil's man.
His lips to my lips to mark all this.

Water Gardening

What could anyone want from the water poppies,
the integuments or the heart-shaped
leaves of the milky-sapped aquatics,
iris and marsh marigold?
What have I wanted from the brown
china marks moth and the ribbon grass,
swamp lobelia and wappato and bee balm? I couldn't
have seen anyone floating
in the tea shadows, spreading
as water mosses, as the brain's pickerelweed.
If I lower myself I can see
the nerves of water, the freshwater whelk's red
jelly eggs, the roots of a flossy lily,
the wind blowing these skins back,
stirring the garden into canals, more nerves, rootlets—
until some gnat-like little botherer rises to pester
my arm and head. He is trying so hard
to deliver his delirium
deliriously, his one eyelash—as if to say,
I can't leave you and I can't stay—of wisdom.

Miniatures

The swans sail outside the glass house of the Netherlands.
The milky child, naked, is about to leap

off her dock. In the sideyard a pear tree is glinting,
the pears so delicate they float

as if a breath might fling them
against the tiny windows.

The ducks are perfectly still.
Their cries—they would sound

like the scratching of papers.
How small a bread crumb would appear.

In a friend's miniatures, life requires
tweezers, a beauteous order

despite his heart, erratic. Erratic too—
more of us, or that one allowing

the world to tell her over and over
of how little worth she is. From distances,

lives may look small. At my home,
strangers arrive in their vast courtship of God.

They want me to join them or else
burn in hell forever. Alone again

---

in the house I feel the presence
of other friendships. These wild flowers

I keep, although wild, last
in their glass captivity, fresh.

One longs for tolerance, what lasts,
how words may come apart in their strangeness

but fall into shapes we recognize.
One may lose certain gestures,

the vocabulary of love, the excited
oh yes a friend gave in toy shops

gone now. She is disappointed today
even in small things. It's quiet now

and different and if I look I see
it is still possible for someone

to cry out like a bird cut from her kind
or once again to enter the glassiness

of time, even as a child might slip into water,
only lifting her head to us for a moment before

streaming through the deep and sparkling
interruption that is her life.

Lee Upton

The Mountain

The first junk to round the Cape
of Good Hope was made of teak.
It passed the improvised dwellings of the poor,

the men huddled around a game
as if it were a fire. A sliver of the teak
is now lodged in glass with the portrait of

the mountain of mountains. That mountain
still dwarfs travelers, the little mules
wobbling under saddles, the monastery,

the young Western woman walking with five
old women whose bound feet scale
the mountain. They surprise her. They are quick.

They wait for the young woman. After a while,
perhaps, the youngest believes, there is no
pain for them. Little specks of earth dance

before the woman's eyes and will not rest
in a world of change,
sudden disappearances, remnants.

These old women—that they still exist—
tottering on claws. They stop
to drink and look down

at a river. It is a silver streak.
As if one hand brushed it upon the earth quickly,
determined to leave everything to chance.

The Debt

A mother shouts for her child Billy.
The shout is like a curse
that has been cracked inside a mouth
for a thousand years.
But the child will return for that voice.
It's what he has after all.

The mother calls
and everyone in the building
must shudder a bit,
that voice, that stick of despair,
making even the oldest remember
how as children they wondered
why they should bother
to learn a new game.

What if that woman shakes her head
and walks inside
and never calls the boy again?
Or no. Here it comes, that voice
like a debt to the world, a debt
of cold and ugly music
necessary for one child.

Bedtime Story

You will stop suffering now and you will sleep,
and the iodine will stop running through your arms and chest,
and your head will rest in the bedtime story of your love,
the little blondes on the dance floor no longer twisting their
backs against your back.
For now drink your very golden beer of sleep,
one bubble rising like the fleck of a musical note
at the corner of your eye.
Remember, if you can, the lovely calamari,
and butter—so much butter,
and the funnily tinny Puccini.
We stared into the street for a while until
it seemed to call to us.
At each moment our risk is our cure.
Stop suffering now and sleep.

Thank You Too Much

Habitually, when I open the door I look for my friend,
although I won't be the one stepping aside
for her small hesitancies anymore.
Now I would like to walk on the lawn,
wanting whatever at long last will occur—
the sheen just beginning to suspend
above blue tiles, the blank little porch.
Whatever gave us our choices?
Earlier there seemed little to choose.
My friend's voice came back
the moment she decided to choose.
I am listening for her now
that she has changed out of an old flesh.
What was so tight for her, what glassed-in?
It is not as if she forever washes a white dress,
although she washed one often enough,
gathering the last of us with her,
some translucent little smear.
She would unlearn anything.
She would not be the one who says, Put your nice dress on,
or, Come down from the city. Yet I think
there could have been something that would please her yet.
She would wash away nothing of whiteness
finally, no dress, nothing of hers.
She said she said the words thank you too much.
But she was always welcome.

Lee Upton

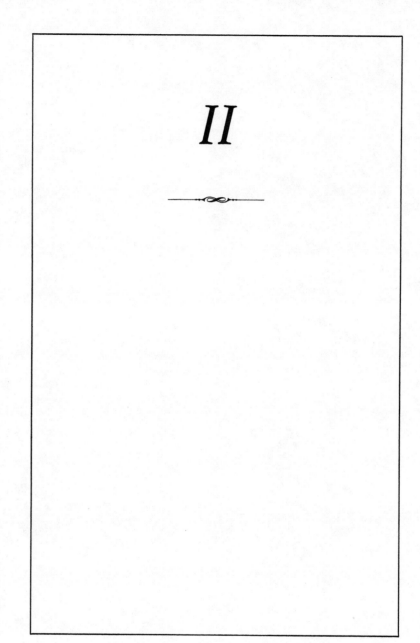

II

Hotel Life

The snow drifts into the window in your dream,
and in your dream the bridge breaks from snow weight.
The nerve patterns of the bedspread seem to break
as you tell me your dream.
But where is the woman standing up from her bath,
or standing away from the red cushions of a chair,
or standing in the doorway and turning
effortlessly as any dream
in a moment when something's about to happen
and no one can be excused?
When I close my eyes I see a friend passing
in a skirt printed with eyes. She wants to know about
your dream of one thing after another
blowing into the room,
and what are these dreams for but fear?
These waterfalls of white peacocks, these lace curtains
strain the day into something sheer
to shut out a little light,
something so that others can't see in.
If we left to put our faces close
to the window of the hotel coffee shop
we would only just barely see
that no one has cleared the tables. There will be
crushed napkins, glasses, and we will want
to know where the owners went, leaving
the old food on the tables,
leaving the whole place a mess.
All this to tell us that they knew enough
to leave everything, that
this is a town far from the sea and that

NO MERCY

you will not change here.
After breakfast your bed, if it is made, will be made
by someone who is late, is told to hurry, but who will
look out the window past the auto dealership
for many minutes at a time, leaving
this life, this hotel life.

Kirsten's Winter Adventure

They know the white horse that pulls
Kirsten's sleigh must not be fast.

A black daub in the distance,
the rider pursuing her has already passed

the icy lake. Full of changes of heart,
winter continues throughout the story:

the runners etching themselves in snow,
the girl's startled face rising,

her timid family unclenching their hands and crying
in their silly, feigned way:

She is gone!
The predictable will never happen to that child.

Needlessly, dramatically, she will suffer
before summer lets loose the small birds

that feed on next to nothing. And the children.
Mine believe they will not be like her.

They think they are small and nervous.
They are only children,

but she was a child of privilege.
She owned a muff, her father

bowed like a gentleman, someone rode
after her. It happened so long ago.

And they who are out of the picture believe
they will never know the rider. Yes,

he is almost out of the picture also,
his head, one blur beyond the snow.

I love him too, I want to say.
I know, I know. I should have

given you names that mean patience,
he won't harm you. Luck, he'll want you also.

Unhappiness

A woman opens the tiny wings of an orange,
the orange so full of juice,
she will not eat it. Instead

the woman has stood to watch the man
in his boat, out so far he appears so small
she thinks she might tear him

from the water with one finger. She stares
as if a piece of God floats off.
She will not turn and look for long

at the men on mats, singing below
the mountain. So many of the artists then
must have seen the world like this:

mossy rivulets, the mountains rounded
by mist. But these pines
are this one's mistake

and diversion. Brilliant as thistle,
they shoot sparks into any eye
that wishes to move to

the singing men, the woman, the boat.
The ink of this world has flown
into the pines. The black songs

of the men below have flocked.
A bird struggling in oil made these.
Anger—before distant water,

the woman's small, indifferent back—
must clot. A great unhappiness
would tell us how feeble

happiness is, how for a moment
we must turn and watch someone
as if we are very calm.

Cleopatra's Spectacle

She took up the truth and it struck her
before those of us who have never so much
as made a scene in public. She behaved

with calm, with attention, as if she weren't
a monster waiting for the perfect friend.
And then she lifted her second truth.

Edward Lear

He weeps by the side of the ocean,
   He weeps on the top of the hill;
He purchases pancakes and lotion,
   And chocolate shrimps from the mill.

—EDWARD LEAR, "How Pleasant to Know Mr. Lear!"

Never can one choose to be
a laureate of restlessness—
and yet we speak a language

with hardly the tipsiest
raft to float upon.
And if at night birds perch

on our topmost hats
our favorite must be
a quivery celestial jelly.

How do we rest upon our little
bobbing rafts? Now a dust
the color of shrimp

lights our rooms. These moments grow
each to each suddenly
precarious

in a summer
when we are turning
to the end of a century

Lee Upton

where there's no hill,
no ocean,
no weeping without purchases.

Hog Roast

If the town celebrates
his roasting
it's their right. He's their hog.
He's pork now.

His life in the mash has gone sour.
The bad fairy presides
over his crispy feet.
The prodigal has come back

and does not need
such company.
Now the fire licks this one all over.
Now the fire is giving its best

hog massage.
Cornfed hog is sweet.
But sweet as a dog
to the prodigal

he's pork now.
And he cannot know better next time.
He cannot cry to the prodigal:
You, little one, shod

in your doubts,
run along to your gorgeous friends!
He cannot cry:
Let me see your back!

Lee Upton

He's pork now.
So we can kiss—if we want—
his blarney lips.
So we're home,

barely edible,
lonely with the whole town.
No one's lonely in hog heaven.
No one's got cooked feet.

Pity for Blondes

When your lithe and secret blonde must leave,
what will you do for yourself?
A blonde does what a blonde must do. She walks on paradox.
A blonde wobbles and falters.
Now your blonde lounges,
a mad mink on a fold-out couch.
The things you don't do for one another could fill a book.

Lee Upton

Jim's Hairball

*Jim got down on his knees, and put his ear against it
and listened. But it warn't no use; he said it wouldn't talk.*

—MARK TWAIN, *The Adventures of Huckleberry Finn*

I said, Jim, let me see that thing.
I said, I wouldn't back away from my fortune, my future.
So I held the hairball in my hands,
and I could feel it wanted to talk to me
with its big thick clots,
its hair from all over,
parts of it as pretty as a walnut.
But at that time
I had been entirely escaping revelation.
I was like a hairworm that lives in running water,
that ignorant, and wanting
the hairball to talk to me
of considerable trouble
and considerable joy,
of two angels batting it out
on either side of my head.
But the thing just sat there
like a ball of infernal knitting.
I wanted to tell it a joke about people,
how we had something in common
with the fourth stomach of the ox
where it came from, to say something like:
Here's how any of us would respond to irritation—
not a pearl but a hairball.
But the hairball just kept looking out at the world

———

NO MERCY

27

like the most compact dusty monkey,
like a terrible eye that saw so much already
it turned on itself, turned into a hard
lifetime of turns and twists.
Now it wouldn't even talk to me for money,
not about drowning or rope or explosion.
Whatever was down in the books
was down in the books
and the books were closed to me.
Jim, I said, How do you do it?
Jim sat back.
Don't you worry, he said to me.
And I said, Jim?
And just like that
we both got on our knees before that thing
and Jim tried, tried so hard
for the last time to teach me *himself*,
and how to learn to listen.

The Quality of Mercy

It is raining—a rain
with a little snow in it.
A woman who begins
by touching a man who is her friend,
those first touches progressing
to the inside of his wrist,
may change her mind
about him in time. Time, too, is your friend—
although for now she has left you.
You lying with her on the bed
in country after country—
that's what you liked best about travel,
talking quietly in a room
after you felt your soul had bled
all day among crowds.
And then wine at an outdoor table, sunlight
on the glass, the world slowing
into a blur of colors, one band of reds.
After the full dream of directions,
the body manipulated into various positions
by the beauty of the world.
To be with her, simply talking,
safe in a room. You remember this
best of your travels and the wife
you begin to forgive. It is
spring and the birds come back
in their gorgeous masks.
The branches on your property are somewhat
red, somewhat pink, in their form
of happy indecency. Mercy

NO MERCY

is more constant than your wife is.
You never want to see her again
but wonder, wonder how she is.
Fine. She is fine.

The Interpreter

The rosy feet of the pigeon are wet,
and the slate roof and the shivery leaves are wet
across the street in the spring rains of Nagoya.
I could drain the rains from my pink blouse
onto the floor—the pink would shred
onto the noodle shop floor.

What I can't say
swims in the noodles that swim in their hot bath.
I miss my friend all the time!

The boy who approaches me to be kind
folds his thin square of paper.
He sits across from me
folding, folding, folding
the paper's thousand years.

And then, at last, late,
filling the whole shop, she's here, my friend,
my translator with her tired face.
All day she has tried to tell the English tour group
that the goddess of mercy
would plant her tiny feet in their hands.

She smiles at the boy who talks to us.
Rising, the boy hands me
the folded paper—flower, bird, boat?
The paper is slippery, a little like the world outside us today.

My friend! Such a poor translator, she says she is
afraid she can never fool anyone.

The goddess of mercy paints on a screen, she said today,
three times, more, but none of the English
understood her. Worse!
She had to write it down.
A woman must wash her face in ink to make a living.
The noodles float, plump, in their weepy little cloud.

If I knew how, I would fold her words into my own mouth.
They would open slowly and I would learn at last
flower, boat, bird as she knows them.
The words that are her perfect ones, that
make the world rise and bob before her.
Mercy on us, I will never have enough mouth and eyes.

Occasional Poem

We do not slit each other's gullets
and cry out
for a pickle of flesh—
with never a tremor—
and it's all and only talk.
Darling, if it's neither here nor there
then where is it?
At the salad bar I look down
and I have no one to tell,
There's mayonnaise all over my wristwatch.
Talk is more than our trouble.
When you don't talk but simply look
I want to cry out, Stop,
my face keeps blowing around.
Talk cannot cheapen you and your race—
and even your aimless aimless chatter is more to me—

New Year's Eve on a Train

We are coming into Kalamazoo
and one of the conductors
is so happy
he sings: Where is the great
train romance
I've been looking forward to?
A friend across the aisle tells me
of writing a letter
on a train in Japan
and five people gathered
just to watch her. For once,
to be a novelty. We
are being taken past
Pudgies, the closed-down sundae shop,
too soon the ice-blue Mattawan water tower.
Someone has decorated his basketball hoop
with Christmas lights, someone who likes
children. The woman beside me
puts down the novel
that promises to thrill her,
its glossy little figure
running off
into the darkness.
Did I tell you that I knew a man
whose nose bled
the first time he put his face
against a woman's breast?
When it happened, he was too young
to laugh or talk of it with her.
Now he wants to remember

Lee Upton

everything. I believe the train
moves to another year
and we can't help
forgetting ourselves.
Slowly everyone becomes friendly—as if we have been
excused from our memories.
I have changed.
Please tell me, Is the same the same there?

III

Invitation to Health

We read as if we read for our lives,
as if we read the story of our bodies,
fever moistening the room
with birds of paradise,
these birds fluttering the pages
of Wilde's *Salomé:*
"I love to see in a fruit
the mark of thy little teeth."
We can hardly talk enough about it,
dancing for promises,
the whole prickly business.
Soon enough we will rise
in the shiny wheel of health,
splashing about among the little devilfish.
And we will celebrate with oysters,
liver and heart and gill,
these Salomés of addled jelly.

We are sure to have our absolute comedy yet.
Neither of us is an Ophelia, flickery as a minnow.
Neither of us a Desdemona drinking her worry tea.
No Electra, crying for a father.
No Salomé swimming through the skins of her dream.
Hadn't we taken, earlier, what we wanted?
Waking with water drops upon our eyelashes?
Each morning cool and slippery as a litchi?
If for now health only waits like a guest
before the grey veins of the window,
we may nevertheless say to her,
our friend and stranger:

Come in. Rest.
Let me give you something to eat.
We'll read to you of Salomé and Minerva,
goddesses of women's work.
Sometimes it is best to swallow,
sometimes to use thy teeth.

Lee Upton

Aide-Memoire

All night the dragon behind you—
you, drinking your sizzling soup—
uncoils out of your head,
the phantom of the gold alloys,
his head, all stuck with stars.
Like the wrinkles of water beneath the cliff,
his skin quivers to light,
his eye, one more sheer drop.
And now here, here
the dragon's complicated golden tail,
the waterfall of his body,
slithers forward.
Every time you bend, his scales flash
and then darken as if all of him,
even the fins on his back,
sharpen within your head.
How was it done once, addressing his kind:
Oh great worm!
This body is marked
with plates the size of raindrops
like the drops that coil
into the drains off the street.
And now because it is the last of winter,
scaly patches of snow are washing away.
We will hear the torrent,
little floes twisting
all the way down to the river. To remember
our night I buy a dragon's egg, blown empty,
hand-painted with gold veins in the restaurant giftshop
where I once saw a chef, blood running down

his forearm, between the webs of his fingers.
He carried his arm as if it were
the arm of a statue he must return.
Out in the parking lot we walk into the night,
the night with drops of rain in it.
The streetlights are all lit
with their pink wetness.
The cars shine like hard candy.
I know that we crouch in the mouth of a dragon, that
he sucks and sucks on us
and we will not be enough for him.
But I forget.
I wear this silly armor.
I am always ready
with so much of my forgetfulness.

Lee Upton

Book of Seasons

Despite the heat of this island
I catch cold
as if a cold
could bring me to that woman
at her window
watching snow.
In her lap I am reading
a book about winter and fall,
a big animal on a path.
The white pages, crisp, flip over.
My hands cover the dark fur.
The snow strays.
But here the sun is opening
festivals. Floats wobble and spray
the sky with red banners.
The schoolgirls stamp
their delicate feet.
At a turn in the dirt a boy
cries outside his father's bar:
Come into our cold place.
Because she is on
the other side of the earth
the woman is asleep,
snow turning upside down
around her.
Difficult to believe
our distance.

The animal, if I recall, is a bear
turning his face toward the reader
in late winter
in a state in the East
which grows increasingly colder.

A Bowl of Shells

This is the one with the tiny nick,
doing penance for some sin. Outside it is aqua,
eggshell thin. Someone walking
down a spiral stair who complains of never
having remembered a dream.
This one is white, thicker-skinned, pearly.
Inside, a tiny civilization once lived, prayed.
And this beauty, so similar, carries a pink dot
at the crown—like a nipple hardened
by the demands of the world.
Inside, mirrors flash.
In this one a bird washes herself,
leaving these prints with her feathers. Here,
the faintest apricot line of watercolor runs,
a long night on a barge and next,
the window that shines and calls us home when
we can no longer be children.
I have one bright yellow one, round.
It reminds me of an infant's head.
This is a minaret where people worship the turtles
in the holy well that fills forever.
In this one the silver mines begin,
and in this other—gold, a sunset
two friends walk toward on a beach
where saints are buried.
This one is an Arabian rug in a fragrant room.
In a corridor,
a mother and child search for one another.
And here is plaster, thick-ribbed with a yellow
inner core. I like the smooth ones best, thinnest,

---

nearest to breaking. They are
too small to make compelling music. They make
less of an effort at pattern, as if each were dipped
into a solution just once, barely.
They are hardly capable of whispering what we might want
to believe is the ocean.
This one with its delicate flukes won't last.
Unendurable, inarticulate. Little grave.
What can they tell me, you, anyone?
Be careful. It's very
early. What we won't give for a well-lit, clean room.
The little throb of the soul scraped free.

Lee Upton
46

Solicitation

I can't tell you about how
they are taking stitches out of my girl's face.
You don't like your small talk, after all.
You don't look at people on the sidewalk.
You stopped going to Jimmy's.
And when my girl hurt her face
you didn't feel a thing.
You might as well say,
I'll see you when I'm dead
or in bed with some disease.
Or maybe once in a while if you're lucky
out with some sack of groceries.
And so when that woman motioned for you to come,
you wouldn't follow her.
And then when you were busted accidentally
for solicitation, run you ran
and you had to regret it.
So when we said,
We thought you died and left us,
and you said, You're right—
I died and left you, how about that,
maybe you should have asked for something.
You should not have said to a stranger,
I'd never be so lonely I'd go
up in a room to eat my money with you.
You don't think you need
one little bit of nice kindness?
What if you add up your zeroes
and go inside yourself then?
You think there's somebody in there, don't you?

What if maybe somebody wants to be alone?
What if you think you have some kind of company
and you're no company at all?
Go. So go ahead.
See. See if somebody's always home.
See if somebody says hello
next time you see your friends.

Destruction of Daughters

The friend who is concerned
with backdrops, not us,
but what we stand against,
his way of looking at the friends
he loves,
to not look at them at all
but at roofs, a bit of sky.
To understand when exactly
a woman is angry
because of the way she works
her mouth
he believes may be enough.
He opens the doors of his house
as the lawn steams with the music
of his daughter.
He has bought a piano
to lure her to him.
The music will never be obsolete,
a vision of the world
in a perfect rain.
As if two friends sat at a table
that suddenly appeared
with wine, the dishes
growing invisible
after they were finished.
And as if a woman spoke—her voice so full of pain
they didn't have to feel pain anymore,
no one, not even that woman,
and such friends
could be direct. All that medicine

for your heart makes you lonely.
Friend, you might as well look
at your daughter
as well as at the air
around her, streaming with music.
The music wants you both but knows
when to wait a little bit,
as if such a daughter cannot help
but be found again,
silent and then crying out, silent
and calling
and is that perfect,
that near a heart.

Sold

I would buy us back,
buy us back
from the auctioneer,
break his gavel and spend.

Each day I'd pay some wage
to buy us back,
buy back that life where
heaven has no uses,

such sad daughters in hoods.
Devil's bait
or angel's,
the devil an angel

and an angel—
I buy. I take back
any feathers,
loaned or owned.

I stay awake
to dark spending,
no thief quite
for that hoard, no

banker, no accountant.
But a bidder,
bidding quickly.
Neglecting no currency,

---

no devil's negligee.
No, no slaves and no slaves'
slaves. We don't obey.
And we pay.

Raw for Plenty

What can move us? What can we dismiss?
What makes us want someone here with us or gone?
I'm raw for plenty—hypothetically. What do I miss?
Tell me your name, when you were born . . .

What makes us want someone here with us or gone?
So long to learn long division, long to learn dread.
Tell me your name. When you were born
lights came to you, a woman took reeds

so long she divided them, divided her dread.
Are you the one I turn another spotted page for?
The lights come on for a woman who reads
your name, a woman who could tell me more.

Are you the one turning pages for
panic, for fear of launching through some abyss?
What name could tell me anything more?
I'm raw for plenty, hypothetical, amiss.

No panic, no fear of launching through an abyss.
What fears come, come to us to be borne.
Hypothetically, I'm raw for plenty. There's someone I miss.
What can move us? What can we dismiss?

NO MERCY

Narratives

Our hero will make a wrong turn.
That's it, always, turning toward one
he cannot love. It's obvious he can
hardly bear to be in the room with her.
I had fallen asleep during their contrived meeting.
When I woke, the fir trees were already
unracking rain.
Drops shone on the railing outside the window.
The thunder stuttered a little,
and a cool wind began lightly touching
everything in the room.
I could always refuse to read to the inevitable,
or let them go, the old forms,
a waterdrop slipping through the ceiling papers.
Perhaps I will not complete certain good works
or return to others. I will never reread
Kidnapped, I don't think.
But I can sit at the window that has stopped
vibrating and know that I am not waiting.
We cannot make the ones we love
come drifting to the very door.

Lee Upton

54

Note in Rain

Rain is all over your note.
The valleys of ink begin to waver
under the pressure.
It is raining on the stone steps
of the museum across the street,
a grey and green rain
that slickens the steps,
slickens too the steps
of the restaurant
where I go for a little clear soup.
It is like drinking rain, but hot and wonderful,
and wondering, Who do you walk with there?
Your mind, does it dance like the papers
when the rain begins?
After two weeks of sickness in the house
it's good for me to leave,
to hear the cold notes of the rain.
Across the street in the museum, I know
that the Egyptian bowls in their parched landscape
are all aware of the rain.
A slight trembling begins among them
and in the blue banners that announce
the Victorian exhibition,
the classifications with
here and there
a grain of grey Victorian humor.
And in the panel the woman you once said
you love wakes,
her black hair growing damp.
She wants to come with us.

NO MERCY

A fingertip passes across the table
she lives near. A little wind
bothers anyone's heart.
Your note didn't tell me how you are,
if your life has changed.
Write again. Visit.
Every face is moist in this weather,
and the museum is so close.

Lee Upton

Happiness

In the hot white dome of air
here where the cicadas scream,
simmer and scream,
as if someone has just put them on to boil,
we take our time with the salesgirl
who has come to our door
with the pictures her brother paints.
A village in clouds,
three people looking at a peach
in a white sky,
a tiny bridge and tinier men.
The title is Happiness she tells us.
She is shy and doesn't expect
anyone to buy anything from her.
In this one
darkness wants to overcome
the awkward shapes on a road,
smudged as if their bodies could
ascend through the firs.
We sink back into the heat,
entering our formless world again.
Her brother paints
all about escape
as if he feels the world
around him too much, more than
the heat on the fourth floor
that presses on us today
but doesn't leave him.
The boy is just learning to paint.
And the salesgirl

in pink tennis shoes,
her head bowed,
wants a glass of water only.
He is sick, her brother, she says.
He spends all day making these.
There's something wrong with him, but
she's not supposed to tell us what.
I take the last scene she shows,
a lion or a yellow bear in snow
and angry at a red bird
above him. If he caught her
he wouldn't let her go.
This animal wants to take
the world in his mouth
and eat it slowly. If he caught her
he would still be angry.
The title of this painting appears,
the painter's sister lets us know,
on the back. It is called Happiness.
She is sorry, she says.
They are all called Happiness.

Lee Upton

ABOUT THE AUTHOR

Born in Saint Johns, Michigan, Lee Upton now lives in Easton, Pennsylvania, where she is an assistant professor of English at Lafayette College. Her first book of poetry, *The Invention of Kindness*, was published in 1984 by the University of Alabama Press. A contributing editor to the *Denver Quarterly*, she received a Pushcart Prize in Poetry in 1987–88. Her poetry, fiction and criticism have appeared in such journals as the *American Poetry Review*, the *Yale Review* and *Field*. She received a Ph.D. in English literature from the State University of New York at Binghamton.

A NOTE ON THE TYPE

This book was set in Garamond, a typeface that was designed between 1540 and 1545 by Claude Garamond and has been a staple of typography ever since. Garamond is one of the first typefaces to have been designed with sixteenth-century printing presses and papers in mind. It no longer mimicked calligraphy but, with its strongly drawn, round letterforms, translated easily from the model cut into metal.